Body Language Secrets:
Babies and Children

D0726804

Other titles in this series
(all by Susan Quilliam):

Body Language Secrets: Babies and Children

Susan Quilliam

Thorsons
An Imprint of HarperCollins*Publishers*

Thorsons
An Imprint of HarperCollins*Publishers*
77–85 Fulham Palace Road,
Hammersmith, London W6 8JB
1160 Battery Street,
San Francisco, California 94111-1213

Published by Thorsons 1996
10 9 8 7 6 5 4 3 2 1

© Transformation Management 1996

Susan Quilliam asserts the moral right to
be identified as the author of this work

A catalogue record for this book
is available from the British Library

ISBN 0 7225 3128 1

Printed in Great Britain by
Woolnough Bookbinding Limited, Irthlingborough

To Desmond Morris – who else?

Contents

Acknowledgements

I would first like to acknowledge the many sources and individuals who helped me gain my research material, particularly the staff of the Open University Library, the staff of the University of London Library, and Felicity Sinclair. A special acknowledgement to Samantha Smeraglia for her ability to collate my research so wonderfully!

My thanks also to: Barbara Levy, my agent, for her continued support; Sharon Scotland, the illustrator; to Jane Graham-Maw, Michele Turney, Jenni Maas and Barbara Vesey from

Thorsons for making the writing and production of this book such an enjoyable experience; to my personal assistant June Bulley for her constant administrative excellence.

A final thank you to my husband Ian who, as always, makes all things possible.

Throughout this book, the people referred to could be either 'he' or 'she'. Consistently referring to one gender would not only raise political issues, but would be unfair to the 'other kind'! In general, therefore, unless to do otherwise would make the text inaccurate, I have alternated pronouns in successive questions in this book, to give a balanced feel.

Preface

Before you read this book, remember that body language:

- is every kind of human behaviour *except* the words spoken – from gestures to breathing, from the way muscles move to a person's use of time
- is not able to tell you everything – you may need the words too
- does not let you read everyone like a book – because everyone has his or her own personalized body language
- will not give you power over people – they will not respond unless they want to

- will not work if you try to change others
  – you can only ever shift what *you* do and
  alter the situation that way
- is about gathering information – you will
  be more successful if you do
- is something you already know – your
  natural body language works best
- is best tried out slowly and carefully – new
  body language patterns can look false
- works by trial and error: do more of what
  succeeds, and stop doing anything that
  doesn't!

How Can Body Language Help Me Understand My Children?

Children are born totally dependent on body language – they simply do not have any other way to communicate. Even after they learn words, they use body language to tell you much of what they want you to know – if only you can interpret it.

So the first way that body language can help in a family situation is to let you understand your children better. By learning just what each of their body signals can mean – the way they stand, the gestures they make, the way their eyes move, the expressions they take on

– you can begin to analyse what they are really saying. You can see beyond the words they use to what is important to them, what they mean to say – and of course, what they are carefully not saying!

But body language is not only vital as an addition to words. Studies show that the vast majority of human communication is not about speech. People succeed or fail because of what their nonverbal signals say – and particularly the impression those signals give. You will want to encourage your children to develop strong and positive body language, so that as adults they give a strong and positive impression of who they are.

To do this, you will not only want to teach the best kind of body language and discourage children from developing bad habits. You will also want to be aware of the signals you yourself are giving, signals that may be providing your children with a negative role model.

Use the three strands of body language together: 1) Understand your child's nonverbal communication; 2) encourage him (or her) in good body language; 3) provide a good example yourself. Of course, all this is not the complete answer to building a happy family. But it will make a great deal of difference.

How Does My Baby Use Body Language Strategies to Make Sure that I Take Care of Her?

When a baby is first born, she is totally vulnerable. If she is not looked after at all, then quite simply she will not survive. And if she does not get consistent care and nurturing, studies show that she will grow up less than fully healthy and well adjusted.

Because of this, nature has sensibly built in certain 'failsafes'. These strategies in a baby's body language and in the ways that adults respond to it make as sure as possible that she has the consistent care of at least one loving adult. These failsafes are geared to work even

when the baby is completely demanding and
totally frustrating, and even when you, the
adult concerned, are tired, stressed and at the
end of your tether.

One key strategy involves appearance. There
are certain body language features that signal
'baby' and which trigger a caring and
nurturing feeling in all adults – though a
slightly stronger feeling in women than in
men. The features, known to psychologists as
'infantile signals', are: a large head in
relation to a small body; plump rounded
limbs; a prominent, bulbous forehead; large
eyes set low down on the face. When you see
them, you automatically want to care. In
fact, this trigger is so strong that humans
have much the same 'aah' reaction to
anything that has these features – a fact that
Steven Spielberg used to great effect when

creating the aliens in *ET* and *Close Encounters of the Third Kind!*

Another key strategy is this: A baby sends out a number of signs that make adults feel that they are approved of – such as turning towards a human voice, and smiling at a human face. Most particularly, baby's pupils dilate – a universal and totally involuntary human movement that signals that the body wants to see more of what it is focusing on. A baby's eyes, however, show this dilation better, because as well as being slightly larger than usual in relation to her face, a baby's eyes have pupils that are larger than normal. All this makes her pupil dilation more noticeable, and the approval signal clearer. Baby signals that she feels good about you – so how can you do anything but feel good about her?

If you are the baby's primary carer, particularly her parent, nature will have built in some further strategies that make you respond strongly to her. Her appearance, for example, will usually create a stronger response in you than in any other adult – one reason why new parents often say that they 'don't usually like babies ... but ours is different.' Her voice will be more recognizable to you than any other baby's; only 48 hours after birth, 50 per cent of mothers in one study were able to identify their own baby's cries from among over 30 others. And if she is in pain or distress, her 'help' cry will produce an incredibly strong physiological reaction in you, so that you cannot resist taking care of her.

The bottom line is that babies may look tiny and vulnerable, but at heart they are simply highly efficient 'adult-trapping' machines!

Does My Child's Appearance Affect His Chance of Success in Life?

It would be wonderful to report that all children are equal when it comes to appearance. It would be great to think that the genetic legacy that a child receives when he (or she) is born has no effect on his chances of success.

Unfortunately, human beings do judge others on essential appearance, and then they behave towards others in response to the way they have judged them. Research has shown that if we think a child is unintelligent, lazy or inferior – even if our only evidence is his physical appearance – then we will treat him that way. And of course, a child will often respond by living up (or down) to our expectations.

So what are the main elements of appearance, the inherited traits that can influence a child's progress? A key one is height: a child who is taller than average or than the other children he is mixing with is likely to be regarded as more intelligent, more competent, more adult. Smaller than average children, on the other hand, may be treated as less intelligent than they are; they may also be teased and bullied more than average, and depending on how they handle this treatment they can therefore grow up to be timid or aggressive.

When it comes to weight, underweight children will often get more attention and be

looked after more than their healthier-looking friends. (Sadly, at even as young as eight and nine years of age, biologically underweight girls will be regarded as more attractive and may be told that they are 'beauties', simply because they fulfil the current ideal of being slim.) Overweight children, on the other hand, will be ridiculed by their peers – up to the age of 11, plumpness is the physical attribute that children actually feel most negative about – and therefore if a child is even slightly overweight he or she can grow up to lack confidence and to feel inferior.

Hair colour in children tends not to influence the way other people treat them – unless they are red-headed, in which case they may well be expected to be quick-tempered, and so possibly will develop this trait. Skin colour, however, quite obviously has a great influence on future prospects, for children as well as adults experience prejudice: Afro-Caribbean children are often stereotyped as lazy and aggressive, while Asian children may be pigeonholed as academic, hardworking and passive.

Equally, anything that makes children appear different will affect them: having to wear glasses, or use a hearing-aid; having a birth mark, operation scar, cleft palette or a squint. All these characteristics will bring out a strong reaction in others, and so play their part in establishing a child's self-image – perhaps making him feel unique and therefore confident, perhaps by making him feel odd and therefore insecure.

There is good news, though. However a child looks, it is his minute-to-minute nonverbal approach rather than his appearance that influences people over the long term. So whatever his natural advantages or disadvantages of appearance, if a child's body language is friendly, confident and intelligent, then he will get ahead.

How Can Body Language Tell Me whether My Child Is Interested in Something or Not?

A child who finds something fascinating has a number of instinctive ways of responding. The result is body language that can easily be spotted, and which will help you identify just when a child is interested and just when she (or he) is bored.

An interested child will first try to get as close as possible to the intriguing object. An infant, who cannot actually move closer under her own steam, will reach out, arms flailing, fists and mouth opening and closing as if she wants to taste the object of her fascination! An older child will lean forward – often tucking her legs underneath her, a body position that even in adults shows interest.

At the same time, there is increased receptivity in all five senses, particularly the two major ones of sight and hearing. A child who is interested in what she sees will raise her eyebrows and open her eyes slightly wider as if to take more in; her pupils will dilate to allow more light to enter so that she can see detail. A child who is interested in what she hears will pull her head up slightly from her shoulders as if to hear better, will tilt her head (because the angle of the jaw has been shown to affect the way sounds are heard), and may well tap out with her fingers or feet the rhythm she is hearing.

A fascinated child will also spontaneously block off other stimuli. Her focus will narrow, so she will take in less of what is happening on the periphery of her vision. Her hearing will become selective – often to the great annoyance of parents, who want their own voices to be heard! She may keep very still, and breathe and move very quietly, as if not to distract herself.

As a child gets older she will also show her interest by 'acknowledgement' signals. She will nod – an almost universal signal of acknowledgement. She will smile the genuine smile which involves not only the mouth but also the muscles around the eyes. She will point, either very noticeably if she is young, or fleetingly and unnoticeably if she is older. She wants you to notice what she has discovered – and she wants you to know just how fascinating her discovery is!

How Can My Child's Eye Movements Tell Me What Is Going on in His Mind?

When a child thinks about something, he (or she) does not just think 'vague thoughts'. A child who thinks about a favourite toy will get an image of what that toy looks like. If he thinks about a favourite lullaby, he will hear that tune in his head. If he remembers the taste of a delicious food, he will re-experience that taste. All their thoughts give children very specific inner pictures, sounds and sensations.

Recent work by U.S. psychologists Richard Bandler and John Grinder has suggested that when children (and adults) think in these ways, they indicate on the outside the sort of thoughts they are thinking. Bodies – and in particular, eyes – move in a way that reflects mental activity.

We already know that children as young as a few months old constantly switch from focusing on what is happening around them to defocusing for just a few seconds. These 'conjugolateral eye movements', or CLEMs as they are called, show that a child is thinking. He is taking 'time out' to store the information he is receiving from the world around him, or retrieving from mental storage banks the information he needs in order to take the next step.

Bandler and Grinder suggest that these eye movements vary according to whether children are remembering something that they have already experienced, or imagining something that they have not yet experienced. Looking to the left, for example (in a right-handed child) indicates a thought that is a memory – such as of the previously mentioned favourite toy. Looking to the right suggests a more creative thought, perhaps putting together several existing possibilities to imagine the favourite toy in a different colour, or possessed with magical powers.

Further, Bandler and Grinder suggest that the angle at which a child looks tells us something about what he is thinking of. An upwards glance often means that the child is thinking about something he has seen – such as that visual image of a toy. A sideways glance will indicate a thought about something heard, such as that lullaby.

Eye movements can only really tell you *how* a child is thinking – in pictures or sounds, in memories or fantasies. They can never give you very specific information – for that you need to talk to your child about his thoughts. But what these movements can do is to help you to ask the right questions to get him talking. So if you see your child looking upwards with a happy expression, you can ask 'what's the nice picture you are seeing in your head?' If you see him looking to the left with a grimace, then you could maybe ask what he is remembering that makes him feel bad.

Interpreting your child's eye movements can give you at least a little more understanding of what is happening in his mind.

What Does Mimicking Me Teach My Baby?

We often tell children off for mimicking other people. But in fact the ability to mimic lies at the heart of children's ability to develop, learn and grow. It is what makes them able to master adult skills and become fully human beings.

Mimicking – or modelling, as psychologists call it – is an instinctive skill for humans. As early as 45 minutes after birth, your baby is able to model an adult doing certain basic movements: opening her mouth, protruding her lips, pushing out her tongue – all of which are necessary if she is going to feed, suckle and prevent

inappropriate food from going in her mouth.
And from this time on she will continue to
model the people around her, imitating
faithfully what she sees, hears and feels
them do.

The driving force for all this modelling is
a love of copying and of being copied. First,
a baby instinctively feels good when she does
something that another person is doing,
particularly if that person is important in her
baby's life. Secondly, of course, if the baby
copies accurately she usually gets a reward from
adults who respond positively, smiling, hugging
or using a delighted tone of voice. And thirdly,
adults themselves often then spontaneously
copy what the baby has done, to reinforce the
message – and the baby then feels good all over
again, because she has the flattering experience
of an adult imitating her right back.

As she grows, a baby will model not only the more obvious nonverbal aspects of human behaviour – such as walking, talking or holding a cup – she will also very accurately model subtle nonverbal pointers from those close to her, such as her parents' accents, their untidy habits or their skill in playing a musical instrument. She will model aspects of emotion and personality, learning from other people's body language how to be irritable, how to be contented, how to be delighted.

This modelling involves nonverbal cues inside as well as outside the body: the baby who screams when her big brother yells at seeing a spider also 'models' his increased heart rate, breathing pattern and the burst of adrenalin that comes with being startled.

All this suggests that encouraging a baby to copy positive skills, attitudes and emotions is not only a good thing, but essential to development. It also, more worryingly, suggests that whether encouraged or not, a child will model regardless. Children growing up in a family where one parent is depressed, for example, have a good chance of themselves 'learning' how to be depressed – whether or not the depression itself is ever discussed or even acknowledged.

You cannot choose what your child models; all you can do is make sure that what you offer her to model is as positive as it can be.

What Should I Do If My Child Will Not Listen to Me?

In most Western cultures, the signs that tell adults that people are listening to them are very specific. Other people look at us when we are talking. They keep still so that they can listen more closely. They nod in acknowledgment. They make little 'mm' sounds to show us that they agree. But all too often, children do not do any of these things. They look away, they do not nod, they do not say 'mm'. They obviously are not listening.

Is this what your child does? If so, begin by quite simply checking whether he actually knows what he ought to be doing. Most children are not bored, distracted or deliberately deaf to what you say; they simply have not yet learned how to signal nonverbally that they are listening. So, finding it easier to listen to your words if he is not distracted by looking at you, your child may not realize that holding eye contact is seen as a sign of respect and attention. Thinking that it is possible to hear and do at the same time, he may move about and fidget. And he may not be aware that 'acknowledgement signals' such as nods and 'mms' even exist, let alone that they are essential.

Can you check if a child is listening or not? The answer, for once, is to ignore his body language and concentrate on his words. A child who, once you have finished speaking, can talk with you about what you have said, ask questions and then act on what has been discussed, has actually been listening. If this is the case with your child, then all he needs is to be taught the body language of listening, and be helped to practise it.

But what about the child who has not listened? One who is unable to respond to what you have said has indeed been paying more attention to other things than to the sound of your voice. Maybe he has been distracted by something else, maybe he has simply been thinking his own thoughts. The answer here is to make yourself more important than other stimuli in order to get your child to concentrate only on you.

The traditional way to do this is to talk more loudly – in fact, to shout. But this often makes the child even more 'deaf'. It is much more effective to use the sense of touch, because touch is the sensory channel with the most direct route to the brain. So go up close to your child, claim his attention with a pat or a hug, then say what you have to say. If you do this, even if he neither looks, nods nor 'mms', the chances are high that he will really hear you.

What Can Body Language Tell Me About My Child's Relationship with Her Friends?

How does your child get on with her friends? You can, of course, tell a lot from the general signs, such as whether other children visit her, play with her, and invite her back to play with them. But you also need to look at more specific body language.

When your child first starts to get close to another child, then both will send out strong 'approval' signals, their bodies' way of encouraging the friendship and bonding with each other. They will be very active on meeting each other, with lots of movement and jumping up and down, as their bodies flood with excited adrenalin. Younger children will smile, laugh, touch – while older children who have learned more adult ways of showing approval may keep their distance, but will still nod and maintain eye contact.

If your child's friendship with another child lasts, then these approval signals will die down as she and her friend feel more at ease with each other. But then the two of them will set out to learn more about each other, on a nonverbal level as well as by talking. They will show each other things, listen carefully and look closely at what the other is doing. Pretty soon, they will be copying, 'matching' body language in very subtle ways, even down to the rate at which they breathe. You may also notice them matching in more obvious ways: buying the same music, wearing the same clothes, playing the same games. This is not just a case of imitation being the sincerest form of flattery. These are also 'tie signs', meant to signal their friendship to the outside world, and to warn other people not to intrude.

If you notice all the above things, then your child's friendship is probably sound. But can you be sure? A child who spends time with others but does not actually like them may smile, because a smile can be faked. But many of the other signals mentioned above will be completely missing; matching of movement, for example. You may also notice secret signals of dislike: signs of mockery such as a hidden sneer, or eyes raised to heaven in exasperation. In particular, if these signals occur when the object of dislike is not looking, or are 'concealed' by the other child putting her hand across her mouth or turning her head away, start suspecting that the friendship is not genuine.

How Can I tell Whether My Child Is Lonely or a Contented Individualist?

It can be worrying if your child seems to be failing to make friends. If he just doesn't mix much when with other children, then how can you tell whether he is happy with this or not?

The essential thing to remember is that some children are happier alone or with just one or two other people. Human company is the most stimulating thing that any child experiences – but it may be stimulating not only in a positive but also a negative sense. Research suggests that some children have sensitive nervous systems, and simply cannot

interact with too many people, too much of
the time. So although your child needs to be
socially competent, he may only be able to
demonstrate that competence when with just
one or two people. In a group, his body may
actually be encouraging him to keep a low
profile.

If you are on the spot, and notice your child
separate from a group, then you can usually
tell quite clearly whether – at least in that
particular situation – he is feeling rejected or
simply wants time alone.

A child who is actively lonely will be slightly
turned towards the group, and will constantly
glance across towards it, as if trying to make
contact. He may play with a toy of his own,
but his movements will be distracted and
hesitant, and he will quickly lose interest and

turn his attention back to the group. He may try to copy the group, from afar, attempting to 'match' posture and gesture but never quite succeeding. In general, he will look unhappy; all the signs are that he wants to be included. Help him to do that by teaching him the skills of getting to know other children and to get along with them.

A child who wants to be alone, on the other hand, will be turned away from the group, and will rarely look up. Instead, he will focus on whatever game he is playing and be seemingly undistractable. He will not copy other children in any significant way because what they are doing is not important to him – or alternatively, if he is playing on his own only for today and normally plays a lot with this group of friends, he will match them spontaneously without even looking. He is perfectly happy and that shows in his easy posture, his half smile, perhaps his little humming sound as he 'talks to himself'. There is no need to worry about this child; he is perfectly all right on his own.

How Can I Help My Child to Be More Socially Competent with Adults?

There are a whole host of body language skills – about how to stand, how to move, where to stand, when to smile, what tone of voice to use, when to touch, when to look – which children need to develop as they grow. These skills are a large part of that complex talent, social competence – and they can mean the difference between success and failure at work, at play, in love and in life.

How do children master social competence? The fact is that eventually most of them do, but it takes a while. They do not get a real chance to practise these rules because they are often discouraged from joining in adult interactions – ironically, of course, because when they do, the fact that they do not use 'normal' body language may make adults feel uneasy.

So why not teach your child lessons that she will rarely receive in any formal learning situation – lessons in how to be socially competent? Most youngsters mature enough to understand what you are saying will be interested to know how they can behave in a way that makes others like them more, and will be willing to try out what you suggest.

Simple rules might include the following:
- Stand near but not too near others, lest people feel uncomfortable – arm's length is about right.

- Do not touch someone unless he or she seems to be reaching out to touch you.
- Do not show it in your facial expression if someone annoys or irritates you.
- Look at people when you are talking to them.
- Smile to show that you like them.

You will want to add a host of other guidelines depending on your child's situation, culture and gender.

Then, rather than simply telling, show your child. You can, when watching television, discuss together what people do that makes them interesting or boring, likable or unlikable; given this chance to be observant, even a normal eight-year-old will almost always spot important nonverbal cues that you miss!

You can bring things slightly closer to home by inviting your child to talk about how she likes or dislikes other people, and what it was about their behaviour that appealed to her or not. When old enough, she will be able to pinpoint that she felt bad because the other person came too close, spoke in a sharp voice, or never looked at her. She will spontaneously report that she felt good because the other person approached to just the right distance, smiled and had a pleasant expression.

As your child learns what works and what does not, she will herself experiment with different approaches. She will try smiling more or less, moving closer or further away, keeping or losing eye contact. Some of these experiments simply will not work, and you may wince – but your child will usually be able to analyse and alter just what she did wrong. Support her not only to experiment, but also to adapt her body language from person to person. In that way she will develop social skills that really work with everyone she meets.

How Can My Child Avoid Being Bullied?

Sneering, laughing, mocking, stealing, beating up – this is not a normal playground tussle; this is bullying. A bully, often unpopular and lacking in self-confidence, wants to hurt, not to fight. He picks on children who do not fight back so that he is never in danger of losing.

The bullied child, then, is one who does not know either how to fight or how to ignore others who try to hurt him. His body language, usually more than his words, signals that he is giving in, that he will not fight, that he is upset by what is happening. The bully reads these signals and sees them as encouragement to carry on bullying, day after day.

If you want your child to avoid this kind of situation, encourage him in the kind of body language that convinces bullies that there is no point in starting trouble. A child who 'walks tall' – who naturally has his head up, who gazes directly at others, whose movements are sure and whose voice is clear and loud – is giving off the signals that, even back in a primitive tribe, mark him out as a fighter rather than a victim. You can encourage this kind of body language, though not, of course, by nagging your child into it. Instead, talk about cartoon characters or television personalities who display these nonverbal signals, and discuss the fact that they would neither fall prey to bullies nor, of course, be bullies themselves.

What if bullying has already started? First, be alert to the signals: a child will almost certainly feel sufficiently bad about being victimized that he will find it difficult to confide in an adult. His body, however, will indicate the problem by signalling stress. Tearfulness, fluctuating emotions, a loss of appetite, a need for much more or less sleep; nightmares; nervous illness – all these, as well as the more obvious cuts, bruises and missing dinner money, are your child's cries for help.

Your initial reaction should never be to blame your child. If you do, he will feel even worse about it all and this will show in his nervous body language, making him even more likely to be picked on. Instead, praise him for confiding in you. Then point out that children who do not get bullied have simply been taught things he does not yet know, in much the same way as he has learned skills that his little sister – or the children in the class below him at school – have not learned.

You can then help your child to develop the following body language strategy, which has been shown to work even with children as young as five. He should 'walk tall', as described above. Then, if bullying starts, he should look directly at his tormentors, telling them in a loud, assertive voice to 'go away' before walking off. The secret is not to be reasonable; it is to act in a confident and aggressive way that suggests that the child will cause real trouble if harried.

Most bullies will stand down at that point because they are not natural fighters. Instead, they will go off and find easier prey.

Why Does My Child Often 'Act Up' When We Are in a Crowd?

Being in a crowd can be an exciting feeling, especially for a child. She sees lots of things, hears lots of noise, enjoys the sensations of lots of bodies around her. As a result, the child's heart rate quickens, adrenalin floods through her nervous system; she feels exhilarated. On top of all that, crowds often act together, moving as one, singing or chanting – human beings like moving in parallel with each other, and the more people move together, the more satisfying it feels.

But a crowd can also be threatening. Seeing, hearing and feeling lots of things at once can send a child into 'overload'. She feels bombarded by all the sensations, her eyes hurt, her ears hurt, her body feels invaded, there are different smells than the ones she is used to. She may feel wary, because humans naturally get scared when unknown or threatening people come too close. Her nervous system responds as if she were being physically attacked, as in many ways she is.

She may try to solve things herself, by reducing the stimulation. A young child may close her eyes and burrow into your coat so she cannot hear the sounds. An older child may go very quiet and still, with drooping eyelids and hunched shoulders.

If this does not work, then a child may
want to work off the tension by movement
– exercise is a useful way to burn off adrenalin
and so reduce stress. But she may not be able
to move – either because the crowd is too
solidly packed, or because you stop her from
running off.

So in the end, the child asks for help in the
best way she knows how – by getting upset.
She may start to weep. She may throw a
temper tantrum. An older child may whinge
or get stroppy. And at this point, her distress
irritates you and she responds to that by
getting even more upset. Within minutes
she is very uncomfortable indeed – and so
are you.

The answer is to be aware of what is
happening for a child who is in a crowd and

to try to reduce the problems. Begin by
making sure that you are as calm as you can
be. A child who picks up your tension will be
stimulated and upset by that just as much as
by the crowd – so keep your body relaxed and
your breathing even.

Next, try reducing all stimulation as much as
possible so that your child does not go into
overload. Perhaps find a place for yourself a
little way away from the crowd, even if this
means sacrificing a better view. If there are
loud noises, block the child's ears. Cuddle a
younger child up, so she feels safe from the
people; stand an older child close to you so
that she is protected from being jostled. If at
all possible, build in breaks: take the child
outside and let her run around for a bit or sit
quietly to recover.

Afterwards, remember that the effects of being in a crowd may take a while to pass off. The child may, in the days to follow, need quiet time in order to balance out the effects of too much stimulation. Give her that opportunity – being in a crowd can be something from which her body takes a while to recover.

How on Earth Can I Motivate My Child?

The nonverbal cues of a child who is not motivated are usually fairly obvious. He will lean back, legs stretched out in front of him as if to distance himself from what is happening. He will turn away and refuse to look; his arms may be folded and shoulders hunched defensively – or he will just stare into space as if wanting to be somewhere else. The whole picture is of a child who is without energy and who simply is not stimulated to do whatever it is he should do.

In physiological terms, though, there is no such thing as a demotivated child. There is only a child who is not motivated to do what you want him to do. If offered something to eat or a game to play, all his internal body responses will change – from weary and lethargic to alert and energetic. Then his external body language will follow suit. He will move quickly and alertly; he will lean forward and focus on whatever he is eager to do. He will have an upturned, lively expression, and a high, fast tone of voice.

How, then, to turn one physiological state into another? Motivation by words can work. The phrases 'extra pocket money ... passing your exam ... not making the football team ... disappointing your friends' may actually alter a child's physiology, speeding up his heart rate, his breathing and adrenalin rate, giving

him the energy to get going. You can also use body language to add extra motivation. Humans are programmed to be stimulated by approval and to shy away from the disapproval of others. Using disapproval or faked approval to motivate can backfire, but unless your child is demotivated to the point where pleasing you is completely unimportant to him, your approval will alter the way he responds.

The most powerfully motivating body language combines all the major approval signals. So if you can do so genuinely, try approaching your child in an affectionate way, looking at him warmly, smiling, nodding, touching him lightly or with a full hug if that is what comes naturally. His mood will improve. Building on that, if you can then show him that more approval will follow if he motivates himself, you may well find that the job that was so difficult now mysteriously gets done.

There is an extra body language strategy, useful for an older child who knows that he is demotivated and actively wants to react differently. Demotivation is characterized by lack of energy, so if your child does something to create more physical vitality, he will often feel more motivated. He could listen to some fast dance music, play a short game of table tennis, run round the garden.

This will not motivate a child over a long period of time. It will not work when the demotivation is based on real disillusionment. But if what is needed is some extra drive to get the last half hour of homework done, then this approach can do the trick.

How Can I Tell If My Child Lacks Confidence?

Confidence signals originally developed in primates. They allowed younger, less-experienced monkeys to signal to those around them when they could do things on their own and did not need help. A confident child, then, is one whose body knows that it can do what is asked of it. The body language reveals that the child does not need help because she looks physically ready for action. Faced with a sports challenge or a forthcoming exam, the child will have a 'ready to go' posture, good balance, sure and easy movement, good muscle tone, a gaze that is

focused on the task in hand, steady breathing and an even tone of voice.

A child who lacks confidence, on the other hand, displays all the signs of physical nervousness. She may seem a little unsure, perhaps with her weight on one foot, or standing with one shoulder higher than the other. Her posture may be slumped as if tired, or rigid as if tense. Her movements may be hesitant and uncoordinated; she may have a worried expression; her gaze may slide sideways nervously almost as if trying to catch someone's eye and ask for help. Her breathing may be skittish, her voice shaky.

You might think that, so far, these signals are straightforward. But children being children, they can vary the signals. A child, for example, who is overconfident will demonstrate all the signals of assurance, but just slightly exaggerated, and slightly speeded up. She will be just too ready for action, too alert, her movements just too quick and eager and her breathing rate just too fast.

And a child who lacks confidence but who is hiding the fact will take the signals to the other extreme, masking any nervousness she might feel with an overcalm posture, too quiet a tone of voice, and a refusal to hold eye contact. Her nerves, however, will show through with fidgets or finger tapping or sudden intakes of breath as the tension builds up.

If your child is completely confident then you will probably simply offer 'touch line support'. If your child is overconfident, you may want to try to get her in touch with the reality of the situation, by first talking slowly and softly to reduce her nervous energy, and then perhaps suggesting that a little more practice might be a good idea.

If you know that your child can really do what she is aiming to do, and that it is only a lack of self-belief that is the problem, then encourage her – using a loud tone of voice. (Not an aggressive one, which will put the child on the defensive.) This is the way that many sports trainers urge on their athletes; it works because the body responds to another person's raised voice by moving into action and simply overriding any lack of confidence.

Once the child has successfully done what she was nervous of, and knows that she can actually do it, then the nerves will disappear and confidence will return.

How Can Body Language Help My Child Cope at School?

A child at school has to learn the right body language strategies for survival. First there are the formal codes, such as raising a hand before speaking and standing up when a teacher enters the room.

Then there are the unspoken rules. These usually involve body control of a kind that does not come naturally to most children: the child must walk rather than run, restrict his movements rather than wave his arms and legs about, keep his voice low rather than shout. He must look serious when he is

working, he must not fidget when the
teacher is talking, and he must not laugh
– unless the teacher laughs, in which case he
must join in.

What if a child breaks any of these rules? Not
only may he get formally disciplined, he will
also suffer much more subtly. He will get less
attention in the classroom and, when he does
get attention, it will be negative and
disapproving. Teachers will consistently speak
to him in a sharp tone of voice, will be less
willing to answer his questions, will mark his
work less positively. The hard fact is that
despite teachers' conscious efforts to give
equal teaching to all, being only human they
will unconsciously respond negatively to
negative nonverbal cues and to the children
who use them.

On the other hand, a knowledge of successful body language will help a child win out in the school situation. For example, it helps to be visible in the classroom. A child who sits at the front or in the middle of the room and seems happy to be 'watched' by the teacher, gets noticed more, talked to more, gets more direct teaching. A child who, having been given permission to talk, speaks out in a clear voice with a confident posture, will be praised more and be given higher marks.

A child who gives nonverbal signals of interest such as an alert posture and direct eye contact is seen as better behaved. If he gives nonverbal signals of agreement and acknowledgement, such as regular nods of his head, he will be seen as more intelligent. These signs have to be genuine, though; just pretending to be interested or motivated may backfire: a false

smile, for example, will result in a very sharp
and negative response from a teacher, who
will see it as mockery.

Does this mean that if a child does not
understand a lesson, he should simply keep
nodding and smiling, and say nothing? On the
contrary, a student who says that he does not
understand is likely to get even more direct
help with his problems, so long as he uses
positive body language. It is only students
who nonverbally show resentment along with
their confusion – seeming distracted, looking
frustrated, chatting with friends – who are
blamed because they do not understand.
A student who uses a puzzled frown, a direct
glance, an attentive head tilt and a quiet,
respectful tone of voice will give the message
'It's not clear – but that's not your fault.'

And that is a message that few teachers can resist – and all teachers will appreciate.

Is My Child's Bedroom Keeping Her from Learning?

How a child learns can be influenced by what the child's body does while she is learning. So if your child's bedroom is the place where she does her homework, studying or project work, then it is worth while making sure that the room is designed to help rather than hinder her.

Does the room provide a focused space for working in? A large room with lots of different areas can tempt the child away from school tasks. On the other hand, does it offer enough space to move in? A child who is starting to get bored can increase her interest

level by simply walking around the room a
few times to raise her heart rate and get her
adrenalin going.

What sort of furniture is there in the working
area? There should be a surface with ample
room to spread out papers. The room should
contain a computer if relevant. And storage
space such as bookshelves can mean the child
is better organized physically, and more
motivated to be better organized mentally.
Put particular thought into the working area
chair. It needs to be high enough to allow the
child to write without strain, flexible enough
to alter as her height does, but not too soft or
the child will tend to snooze rather than
study. The chair also needs to support the
child's back without making her slump and
so compressing her internal organs in a way
that may be unnoticeable but will

84

nevertheless reduce her level of
concentration.

What about the noise level? The myth is that
any noise makes it more difficult to
concentrate, and certainly loud noise will stop
a child from being able to think. Interestingly,
though, many children cannot work in
complete silence, so there may be an argument
for allowing some background instrumental
music – which can stimulate the body and
keep the mind alert.

Is the lighting sufficient? Very dim lighting
makes concentration difficult because its 'near
twilight' convinces the child's body that it is
time to sleep, while very bright lighting can
make the child so active that she wants to
move around rather than sit and work.
Instead try a darkened room with a single

spotlight, which may make the child less likely to move and talk, while at the same time focusing her attention on what she is doing.

Is the room warm enough? Too cold, and all the child's body energy will go into keeping her warm; too high a temperature can create drowsiness; too regular a temperature dampens spirits. The answer may well be heating plus a slightly open window!

The bottom line is that if her surroundings are supportive, a child cannot only learn more quickly and effectively – she will also enjoy her learning far more.

How Can I Help My Child to Develop Emotionally?

Emotions are the way the human body signals that something we are experiencing is important – whether that experience is a real event or a thought about a real event. The body stirs up a whole host of inner physiological reactions that prepare us to cope with what is happening.

These emotions, and their physical reactions, vary according to what the event is. So, for example, if an event is important to a child because he feels threatened by it, then he will experience those reactions as the emotions we call 'fear' and 'anxiety'. Perhaps he will feel cold as the blood rushes protectively to his internal organs, get butterflies in his tummy, tremble a little, curl slightly forward as if to protect himself. If what is happening seems to suggest that he must fight back, then he may feel 'irritation' or 'anger'; he will automatically tense as if ready for a fight; he may feel a rush of adrenalin to prepare him for the attack; his heart may beat faster.

If he needs outside support because of what has happened, we call this 'grief' or 'sadness'. He will signal his need for help with a posture that droops, with a downcast expression and tears. He may feel heavy inside, his eyes will fill with tears, his mouth will spontaneously turn down with a trembling lower lip, his body will droop just slightly. And, of course, if what is happening

is wonderful, then he will feel a rush of positive energy in his body, he will move, smile or laugh with happiness and excitement.

A truly balanced person feels a range of emotional responses and can recognize and offer support when other people feel emotions. A child's ability to do this develops, given the right encouragement.

To help your child to develop emotionally, the first step is to get him to realize that he has actual physical reactions to significant events. Ask how he is feeling inside when he seems to be sad, irritated or excited. Tell him how you feel when you yourself get upset, angry or ecstatic. Create an emotional vocabulary with which he can describe these sensations – perhaps 'shaky' or 'wavy' for anxiety; 'burning' or 'thumping' for anger; 'fizzy' and 'bubbly' for happiness.

You can also help your child to recognize the external signs of emotion. Talk about how he himself naturally expresses them – by crying, shouting, shaking. Discuss how you express your emotions. Look at how other 'real' and 'pretend' adults on television express their feelings. Get him to watch people's eyes, eyebrows and mouths, which are the key ways that most people signal their emotions.

And as he grows, help him to gain empathy. Talk about how sad he feels at another child weeping, how he wants to offer a hug when another child is frightened. The final aim is to develop in him not only a recognition of emotion, but a real skill at being able to support others when their feelings are painful or unhappy.

What Is 'Incongruence' and How Can It Turn My Child into a Monster?

Human beings feel a number of emotions, all the time. Although we are not aware of it, our bodies are constantly reacting to events with tiny flutters of anxiety, euphoria, surprise, irritation. When this happens, different parts of our bodies react in different ways. Stimulated by different emotions, they produce different sensations and different body signals. Normally this is not a problem. Our emotions, and their physiological indications, co-exist quite happily.

But sometimes these emotions conflict. Particularly, if children are told as they grow up not to feel certain feelings, they may experience emotions that seem to fight each other. A boy told that it is unmanly to cry, or a girl told that it is unfeminine to be angry, will desperately try to control these feelings. They will try instead to feel courageous or calm, will find themselves with a physiological battle on their hands between two sets of emotions – and then add to the problem by panicking because they cannot control their feelings. This is called 'incongruence'.

The way incongruence feels to a child is, quite simply, awful. The child's nervous system experiences first one thing, then another, flooding her body with different sensations from one moment to the next. The child feels energetic one minute, tired the next; she

throws a temper tantrum, then dissolves in tears. The child feels terrible – and so do you.

The body language signals that a child displays when she feels incongruent are also problematic because they contradict each other. If, for example, a child starts to get angry but then gets frightened of her own anger, she may speak quietly but act violently; her fists may clench but her mouth may smile; the right side of her body may signal 'furious' while the left side signals 'scared'. The result is a child whose nonverbal signals are a mixture of different emotions – so much so that she confuses and irritates everyone who meets her. Studies have shown that a child who tries to hide anger under a mask of friendliness is seen by others as much more 'untrustworthy' than a child who simply gets angry, but then recovers.

The secret of coping with an incongruent child is to acknowledge the incongruence and bring it into the open. Explain that you often have conflicting emotions yourself – perhaps feeling irritated, guilty and defensive all at the same time because you scratched the car. Then when your child feels the same about breaking a toy, she will be less likely to panic and tumble into a spiral of incongruence.

If she does, give her the opportunity to talk things through. A child who can express all her feelings while you offer a listening ear and a hug will be far better able to cope with the sensations her body is experiencing. She will be better able to acknowledge her mixture of responses. She will calm down more easily. And, in the end, she will learn to understand what she is feeling and so control her emotions much more effectively.

How Can I Best Support My Child When He Is Feeling Down?

If your child is unhappy, the most basic comfort you can offer is the kind that takes him back to the earliest days of his life – back to the womb. Then, there was warmth. There was secure touch all round its body. There was regular movement as mother moved around. And there was rhythmic sound as mother's heart kept beating.

This is why, to calm babies, mothers instinctively wrap them firmly, rock them, sing them lullabies. Tightly wrapped or 'swaddled' babies are physiologically more

relaxed; they have a slower heart rate and steadier breathing. Babies who are rocked, walked or patted – as long as the movement is slow enough to recreate the 70 times a minute of the normal mother's heartbeat – calm down more quickly. Babies who are sung soft, rhythmic lullabies – which also recreate the soft, slow beat of the heart – tend to fall asleep more easily and quickly. And it is no coincidence that 80 per cent of mothers, when they pick up their babies, instinctively hold them on the left side with baby's ear next to their heart.

An unhappy older child cannot actually be swaddled, but you can adapt many of these early comfort reminders to soothe him. If he is not happy to be held, try a blanket or warm sweater round his shoulders. If he is happy to be held, give him a firm hug, one that

embraces as much of his body as possible.
Rock slightly backwards and forwards – some
children will spontaneously start rocking
themselves when they are upset – and perhaps
even add a rhythmic patting or a comforting
murmur. If you can, pat or murmur in time
with your child's crying or breathing, then
gradually slow down. You will find that your
child's sounds and movements will become
calmer too.

Let your child say when the hug should end. If
you move away, what you are saying is 'pull
yourself together' – not a comforting message
for anyone who is unhappy. In fact, given
time, all children will spontaneously 'flop' or
wriggle as a sign to you that they have had the
body contact they need. When you get this
signal, let go, though you may want to
continue to offer your child contact – a hand

to hold, an arm round his shoulder, a touch
on tummy or back (where many children feel
tense).

You should be able to tell, through his body
language, when your child calms down and
cheers up. He will straighten his posture, start
focusing on things, look up and round the
room rather than down as if into himself – all
nonverbal signals that he is starting to become
aware of the outside world and is ready to
interact with it again.

He may want a final hug or pat, as a mark of
the change from comfort time to action time
– but a few minutes later it will be as if
nothing happened.

Is There an 'Instant Body-language Fix' for a Young Person Who Is Emotional?

Sometimes, a young person needs to have a way of calming herself that is instant and reliable. She has a row with a friend just before school; she feels anxious before an exam. Being comforted, talking the experience through, making sense of what has happened – all these will come later. Now what she needs is instant self-control.

This body language strategy works best with children who are old enough to recognize that they do sometimes feel emotional, and mature enough to want a way to cope with that. It will not work with a child who is so young that she always needs outside help, or who is not really motivated to cope alone. The strategy needs to be explained, discussed, taught and rehearsed before it will work spontaneously – and the child has to know that whether or not she does succeed in using the strategy to calm herself down, you will still love her when she gets back home!

The key is for the child to spot the very early signs of distress. These might be of anger – for example, a first rush of rage across her chest; of fear – her stomach may churn with anxiety; or of unhappiness – tears well up. If she has spotted these signs, her body will already be mobilizing itself for action in the way described on page 88. She therefore needs to do two things: first, let her body move into action, in order to reduce the physical symptoms that are making her feel bad; secondly, distract her mind from the body's signals by giving it other things on which to concentrate.

To begin with, the child needs to move about. She should get to her feet and walk or run; if in class, she may need to leave the room so that she can do this. Once she is moving she should try to keep her posture straight and her head up – physiologically this stops the body from, quite literally, sinking into a more 'depressed' state. Research has also shown that looking directly upwards reduces pain, so if the child feels strongly uncomfortable or unhappy, she could try tipping her head back and looking at the ceiling.

While she is doing this, she can start to focus her mind away from the problem that is upsetting her. She could do some simple but involving physical activity such as patting her head and rubbing her tummy at the same time. Or she could do some simple mental activity, such as saying a times table or trying to remember the names of all the children in her class. Decide in advance with your child what she could do, otherwise she may be too upset to think of anything, and then may just give up.

In a short while, the child will start to sense that her mind is clearing and that she is more aware of what is going on around her than of the emotions she is feeling. A good way to complete the process is to take three deep steadying breaths – before carrying on with what she is doing.

How Can I Tell If My Child Is Lying to Me?

Even the nicest child can twist the truth sometimes – and at a very early age. Thankfully, it does not come naturally; it is as if a child's body responds strongly to his saying things that his mind knows are not true. So if you can spot the very first signals of truth-twisting, and challenge those signals, you can often nip the problem in the bud.

The body of a child who is being 'economical with the truth' will send out signals of anxiety and nervousness, usually the ones he normally uses when he is worried. He may use little 'escape' kicks of the feet, little fretful gestures of the hands. The child's body may be stressed, with a rigid trunk, tense jaw, clenched fists. And because this stress is triggered directly from the nervous system, it may also manifest itself as stuttery breathing or a sudden flush of colour to the cheeks.

These anxiety signals are not proof that your child is lying. They only reveal that he is nervous – which he will naturally be if you are accusing him of not telling the truth. But when you see these nervous signs combined with 'camouflage' signals, then you may start to be suspicious.

So beware the small child who turns away from you so that you cannot see his face, one who covers his face with one hand or puts his head down behind a bent elbow. Watch for

the older child who suddenly goes very still, 'blanks out' his face as if wary of showing any expression, who cannot look you in the eye, or who blinks constantly when he does look. Be wary of the child who looks overconfident, holds your gaze unnaturally, or gives you an overbright false smile that does not quite reach his eyes. All these signs may mean that he is trying to hide from you the fact that there is something very wrong.

A final group of signals to look for are those that indicate that the child's body is actually trying to halt the lie in midflow. He may put his hand to his mouth, as if to stop himself speaking; he may bite his lip; he may drop his head and mumble the words so that you will not 'really' hear them. His voice may sound slightly different, higher in pitch; studies have shown that the actual voice box may close up slightly when we are being false, as if literally trying to keep the lie from being spoken.

To challenge a child you suspect of lying, the secret is to move in close. Look into his eyes, even if you have to bend your head to do so. Grasp his hands. Unable to hide behind a barrier of nonverbal camouflage, he will be far more likely to tell you the truth. When he does, signal clearly in words and hugs that you are pleased he has done so – even if you then punish him for originally lying. If your child learns that telling the truth is inevitable and gets him rewarded, then he is far more likely to take the honest route next time round.

How May My Child Use Body Language to Try to Solve My Partnership Problems?

Even if you do not tell your child that there are difficulties in your partnership, she will spot them, from you and your partner's body language. She will also react with her own body language. But what if, as with many family problems, talking about the issues is taboo? Then body language may be the only way that your child can communicate with you about what is happening.

One strategy she may use is to try to ignore everything – so that it will go away. She may seem to become selectively deaf or even

blind, not noticing rows or tears. This
strategy of 'filtering out' problems can
affect her more general body language.
Children in stressed families may develop
hunched shoulders, as if blocking out what
they hear. They may start to avoid eye
contact, as if blocking out what they see.
They may develop a drooped posture, as
if concentrating on themselves rather than
having to notice what is happening around
them.

Alternatively, your child may reflect the
problems rather than ignore them. Faced with
anger, anxiety and grief in the family, the
child becomes a mirror of any or all of these
emotions. She does the fighting, being tense
and aggressive, hitting out at school or at
home, using a fast, irritable voice. She does
the worrying, becoming suddenly less

confident, with hunched posture and nervous movements.

The child may also use body language aimed at stopping your problems by having worse problems of her own. A child may start stealing, swearing, being violent. Or she may become accident prone or ill. What is happening to her may be so painful that you and your partner are forced to take notice and, for the moment, put your own difficulties aside. Your child's body is trying to bring the family back together – whatever that cost.

Or the child may take sides in order to defend one partner and reject the other. She may start behaving aggressively towards one of you, hardly speaking, being rude, using a hostile tone of voice and angry movements. At the same time she may be extremely comforting to the other, with hugs, smiles and attention. The aim is to push the situation to a conclusion by backing one partner and driving the other away – or by supporting one partner in order to get the other to stay.

The solution to all these problems may well not be in your hands. You may need support, from family, teachers or maybe even a counsellor, to reduce your child's strain at the same time as reducing your own family difficulties. The key, however hard it seems, is to break the silence and acknowledge what is happening. If you can allow your child to talk – to you or to someone else – about what is worrying her, then she may not need to express her feelings through body language any more.

What Body Language Do I Use When I Discipline My Child?

Discipline does not just mean telling a child what or what not to do. Controlling your child begins long before he understands what you are really saying. The basis is the body language you use – which signals to your child what you feel about what he has done – and which aims to make him feel so unhappy that he will never err again.

Basic discipline signals show your disapproval. You will almost certainly give these signals naturally, looking at your child with what is called a 'minus' face. You will stare

confrontationally, down your nose, with a
frown, a negative shake of your head and a
strong, irritated tone of voice. The nonverbal
message here is that the child has done wrong
and you therefore do not approve of him; it is
a very powerful message for children to
receive – so much so that some research
suggests that if you start using it early enough
in life, then later, simply shaking your head or
frowning at a child who is about to do
something forbidden will get the effect you
want.

If a child has done something really naughty,
you may want to use stronger body language
signals. These exaggerate non-approval signs;
your voice is louder, your stare more fixed,
your movements fast and energetic. As a
short, sharp shock, this angry approach can
work well; it shows the child that if he does

something wrong he can expect an immediate and negative reaction. But of course, you should never let your aggressive signals spiral into aggressive action. Whether or not you should smack your child is a matter for debate, but if you do, then it should be in a controlled rather than an aggressive way. If you are tempted to violence, leave the room immediately and only return when you are calmer.

There can be a temptation, particularly with an older child, to try to combine stern words with friendly and reasonable body language. The problem here is that research shows this approach to discipline to be the one children least respect. It confuses and angers them because they know that it is emotionally dishonest and they rebel more easily at a later date.

Another problem occurs when you punish some behaviour which you secretly find amusing or clever. Your words and tone of voice may be stern, but there is an amused smile lingering round your lips and your eyes – and your child will spot it. The message will be not only that what he did was acceptable, but that in future your disapproval should not be taken too seriously.

Whatever approach you take to discipline, link punishing body language very directly with the forbidden activity. Once the child is behaving again, revert immediately to your normal, approvingly-smiley self. If you do not, then the punishment will lose its effect – not only because the child will feel that nothing he does will ever bring an end to the punishing behaviour, but also because he is not being rewarded nonverbally for 'being good'.

How Do I Know If My Child Is Really Repentant?

A child who is truly sorry will display body language signals that actually parallel animal appeasement signs. She will hold out her hands – or offer to shake hands – in the age-old way that humans have of showing that they are not going to hit you and that their hands are free of weapons. She may dip her head in another age-old signal that shows that you are in charge and she is not challenging you any more. She will be quite happy to be hugged and touched, and will abandon herself to that because she knows that the worst is over. To make amends, she will stroke your hair, face or clothes, as if grooming you – a younger child may actually cling to your clothes just as a baby chimp does to its mother's fur.

But if the apology does not come from the heart, there will be very different signals. If your child is saying sorry only because you have told her to, then there will be some anger underneath the words; look for tiny signs of rage, such as gritted teeth, clenched fists, or a tight hard voice. If she thinks she is fooling you in some way by apologizing, then there will be a mocking smile lurking underneath her serious face, and a sideways glance as if to invite other people to see how clever she is being. And if you are affectionately forgiving, and want to hug her, she may go stiff and unyielding, because while you may now feel close enough to

touch she knows that there is still aggression
between you.

You cannot actually challenge this behaviour.
If you do, the child will just keep insisting she
is sorry, and you cannot prove her wrong. But
for your part you can at least be sure that you
are not providing her with a bad role model. If
adults apologize because they have hurt or
ignored a child's feelings, often their body
language undermines that apology. So if you
say 'sorry' in a low voice that does not really
want to be heard, accompany the word with a
sharp tone of voice and an irritated gesture,
and make light of it with a mocking tone or a
jokey gesture – then the message your child
gets is that apologies are not really important.

Instead, take it seriously. Sit or kneel so that
you are on your child's level to give the

message that you are not patronizing her. Maintain good eye contact to show that you want to reach her. Then use a slow, measured tone of voice that says you are taking this apology seriously.

Most children, when given such genuine repentance, will react with a forgiving hug or smile. More importantly, they will learn how good it feels when another person makes amends. Knowing that will make it much more likely that your child will be willing to return the favour next time she is in the wrong.

Why Has My Wonderful Child Turned into a Horrible Teenager?

Some young people do seem to 'go off' while they are passing through the phase from childhood to adulthood. At ten, your child wants to be with you and likes your company. He hugs and kisses you, smiles and chats to you.

By 14, he seems to avoid you as much as possible. He stops all the formal signs of being close to you, such as hugs, kisses or snuggling up on the sofa. He turns away from you, rarely keeps eye contact, hardly ever smiles. He hides away in his room, with 'keep off' notices on the door. And when in company he will not interact, speaks in an angry or flat voice, and gives off signs of absolute hostility that make him almost impossible to live with. What on earth is happening?

One explanation of this, in body language terms, is as follows. As a child, dependent on parents, it is appropriate for a young person to use body language that bonds him to his parents, brings him closer to them and makes everyone in each other's company. Hence the natural smiles and snuggles.

But adolescence is all about gaining independence. Not only are young people going through all kinds of physiological changes – involving hormones and genitals, periods and wet dreams – which make them unsure and nervous about how others see them; teenagers are also redefining themselves as separate from the adults in their family. And so, even if just for a short while, their body language has to make the break.

Particularly if the teenager feels unsure of his own ability to be independent, his body may put up barriers to stop him staying too dependent on his parents. His body language reflects this first by cutting down on bonding behaviour such as touch and eye contact, and secondly by putting up hostile barriers, such as a brusque tone of voice and 'keep off' notices on his bedroom door.

What can you do if your teenager behaves like this? The answer, in all honesty, is to wait it out. Most young people will come back, given time and the opportunity to make contact when they need it. Once they are sure that they can handle being independent adults, they can allow you back into their lives once more. They will start looking you in the eye, smiling and chatting, even offering a hug or a kiss.

Your horrible teenager will, as if by magic, turn into a socially competent and really very likable young adult!